Hello there!

Welcome to YETI: A MONSTER KIDS GUIDE! Your key to unlocking an ancient Himalayan Mystery!

This indispensable book informs its reader of the history, folklore, evidence, and adventure surrounding the hunt for that affectionately named Abominable Snowman, better known as the YETI!

It includes locations of some of the best Yeti hotspots in the Himalayas, advice on monster hunting equipment, famous sightings, compelling evidence, and the best times and conditions to spot this shy and elusive beast!

Whether you're simply curious about the legend of the Yeti, an amateur monster hunter, or even plan to visit the Himalayas, this guide is perfect for you. Whether you choose to hunt the Yeti in the field or from the comfort of your own home, this pocket-sized-pilot is designed to enhance your experience, making it a versatile companion for all!

Will you be the one to prove the existence of the legendary Yeti?

Good luck!

A Brief History...

The Himalayas are an immense Mountain chain that stretch 1700 miles, from Afghanistan in the west to Assam in the southeast. They straddle six countries and boast diverse tropical valleys, alpine forests, bleak slopes, and glacier-topped mountains.

Legend has it that among the enormous variety of wildlife that inhabit the Himalayas, there may also be a population of giant, unknown apes known as - Yeti.

The Name *'Yeti'* comes from a Sherpa word pronounced "yeh-tay". It is generally understood to mean *'Rock animal,'* with Yeh meaning *'Snowy Mountain'* or *'Rocky Area'* and Teh meaning *'Animal.'*

A Brief History, cont'd...

In the culturally diverse region upon which the Himalayas sit, the Yeti is known by many names, such as *Banjhankri, Chelovek Medvied, Chelovek Mishka, Chu-Mung, Dre-Mo, Dzu-Teh, Jungli-Admi, Khya, Metoh-Kangmi, Mi-Chen-Po, Mi-Go, Mi-Teh, Osodrashin, Pi, Rakshi-Bompo, Samdja, Snezhniy Chelovek, Sogpa, Yah-teh, Yeh-teh*, and of course, the eternally loved and forever fun – *Abominable Snowman!*

Fun Fact: The Yeti has two scientific names! *'Homo Nivis Odiosus'* - meaning *'The Abominable Snowman'*, given by mountaineer and explorer Maj. Harold T. Tilman in 1937; and *'Dinanthropoides Nivalis'* - meaning *'Big man in the Tundra'*, given by renowned cryptozoologist - Bernard Heuvelmans in 1958!

But is the Yeti real? Let's examine some of the highs and lows of Yeti hunting over the years and see if we can convince you!

Hunting the Monster

The advent of Yeti-mania started with Michael Ward's photograph of an alleged yeti footprint found on the Menlung glacier during Eric Shipton's Everest Reconnaissance Expedition on November 8th, 1951.

Since then, the quest to uncover the truth about the Yeti has been a rollercoaster of highs and lows. From expeditions led by intrepid adventurers to scientific investigations, the search for the Yeti has captivated the world.

However, this shy and elusive creature has always stayed one step ahead of its would-be capturers!

A Prehistoric Relict?

Unknown Anthropoid Ape: Could an undiscovered ape from the same genus as the orangutan, or similar to the extinct Miocene ape – *Sivapithecus,* exist in this sparsely populated region?

Monster Imposters: over the years, believers and sceptics alike have proposed a diverse range of creatures as possible Yeti imposters. These include the Asiatic Black bear, the Himalayan red bear (a subspecies of the brown bear found in the western Himalayas) and the Tibetan blue bear (one of the rarest bear subspecies in the world). Some even suggest that sightings of the Yeti could be caused by monster-sized Macaques, wandering monks, or even the mythical 'yaksha,' a hairy being known from Sanskrit texts that is said to possess superhuman strength!

A Zoomorphic Deity?

Between two worlds? Could the legend of the
Yeti represent the religious superstitions of
Lamas and Sherpas that were misunderstood
by impressionable Western tourists keen to
learn about the folklore and esoteric cultures
of the Far East during the late 19th and early
20th centuries?

During Sir Edmund Hilary's 1960 Himalayan
Expedition, he concluded that Yeti sightings
made by Sherpas were unreliable because
they did not distinguish between the
supernatural and the natural world.

Was he right, or did his Western mind fail to
understand a culture that believes these
creatures inhabit both worlds
simultaneously?

What to look for...

Eyewitnesses describe a large muscular creature measuring approximately 7 feet 6 inches tall, weighing between 200 and 400 pounds, and covered in thick dark greyish-brown, reddish-brown, or black hair.

It has a pointed head with deep-set eyes, a flat nose, and a wide mouth with large teeth. Its arms are ape-like, with large hands and long fingers reaching down to its knees. Its legs are also ape-like and bowed.

Its feet are plantigrade, measuring between 8 - 13 inches in length and 4-6 inches in width. Its large big toe is separate from the other four.

When to look...

Debunked: Contrary to popular belief, the Yeti's preferred habitat is not the high mountaintops but the forests that lie far below the snowline. It is most commonly spotted at dusk or dawn, blending into its surroundings.

Fun Fact: According to local lore, the Yeti only ascends the snowfields, from 10,000 to 23,000 ft., during autumn, in search of food.

Important Tip: The best location to find a Yeti could depend entirely upon the season!

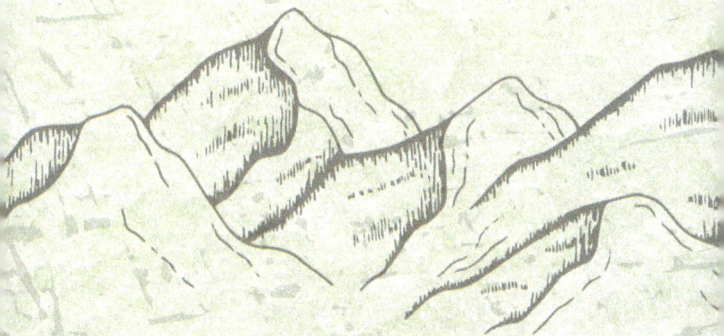

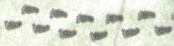

How to look...

There are many ways to search for the Yeti, such as booking a sherpa-guided trip on one of the many mountain treks available around the Himalayas or staking out a popular Yeti hotspot.

Certain tools are needed when attempting to gather viable evidence of the Yeti. These include a high-quality pair of binoculars, a camera with a telephoto lens, tweezers, latex gloves, and an envelope for handling potential biological samples. Also, a can of minimally expanding insulating foam, two pieces of cardboard, a small brush, and a paperweight are invaluable for quick, lightweight track casting!

Remember! Success depends upon preparation; and without preparation, we may never capture proof of this shy and elusive animal!

Where to look...

The Yeti is reported throughout the Himalayan Mountains of Nepal, Kashmir, India, and Bhutan; the southern Tibetan Plateau; southern Xinjiang, Uygur Autonomous Region of China; and Northwestern Yunnan Province, China.

That's it... now you have all the information you need for a successful sighting.
Good luck on your Yeti hunt!

Where to look, cont'd...

Here are some crucial historical sighting hotspots that you should definitely check out!

Remember to mark the places you've been, online or in person. Your contribution could help further our understanding of this mysterious creature!

☑ I was here
☑ I saw a Yeti

Brian Houghton Hodgson
Nepal...

In 1832, Brian Houghton Hodgson, the Court of Nepal's first British Resident and the first Englishman permitted to visit this forbidden land, recounted a chilling encounter that his native hunters had with a *wild man*, saying:

"My shooters were once alarmed in the Kachár by the apparition of a 'wild man', possibly an ourang, and fled from it instead of shooting it. It moved, they said, erectly, was covered with long dark hair, and had no tail."

☐ I was here _____

☐ I saw a Yeti _____

Tombazi Sighting -
Zemu Glacier, Sikkim State.

In 1925, photographer N.A. Tombazi found fifteen small footprints at a spot where he had seen a naked, bipedal, human-like figure walking shortly before.

Tombazi discovered the tracks while hiking near the Zemu Glacier in Sikkim State, India, at an altitude of almost 15,000ft.

Tombazi described seeing a: *"tall, naked figure tugging at rhododendron bushes."* He added, *"It appeared dark against the snow and, as far as I could make out, wore no clothes!"*

☐ I was here
_____

☐ I saw a Yeti
_____

Major Bill Tilman -
Zemu Glacier, Sikkim State.

Bill Tilman, considered the greatest explorer of the twentieth century, earned the nickname "The Original Indiana Jones."

In 1938, while ascending the Zemu Glacier in the Kanchenjunga range, Tilman discovered a trail at about 19,000 feet. His Sherpas believed it led to the lair of the legendary Yeti!

This discovery was particularly striking as it coincided with sightings by photographer N.A. Tombazi in 1925, who reported footprints and a strange figure in the same area, adding to the Yeti legend

☐ <u>I was here</u>

☐ <u>I saw a Yeti</u>

Mingmah Encounter -
Pangboche, Nepal.

In March 1949, a shepherd named Mingmah was tending his yaks in Pangboche, Nepal, when he heard a loud, terrifying noise. He turned to see a Yeti and, in fear, hid inside a nearby stone hut.

Through a small opening, he watched the creature walk on two legs and growl at him.

In a bold moment, Mingmah grabbed a smoldering stick from the fire and attacked the Yeti, causing it to flee.

☐ <u> I was here </u>

☐ <u> I saw a Yeti </u>

Colonel John Hunt -
Khumbu District, Nepal.

During a 1953 expedition, Colonel Hunt and his team visited Tengboche Monastery to meet the local abbot.

While there, an elderly monk told them about a Yeti sighting a few winters earlier. He described the creature as about five feet tall, covered in grey hair, and moving on both legs and all fours.

The Yeti had been playing in the snow before, but it was scared away by the sound of conch shells blown by the monks.

☐ <u>I was here</u>

☐ <u>I saw a Yeti</u>

Tensing Encounter -
Phortse Trail, Nepal.

In December 1950, Sherpa Sen Tensing was traveling from Tengboche to Phortse when he spotted a reddish-brown yeti in the moonlight. Hiding behind a boulder, he watched as the mysterious creature passed by just 25 yards away.

Discover the beauty of the Phortse Trail and visit highlights like Phortse Sherpa Village, the Khumbu Climbing Center, or Tengboche Monastery.

Who knows, you might even cross paths with a Yeti!!!

☐ I was here _____

☐ I saw a Yeti _____

Sonam Hisham Sherpa -
Namche Bazaar, Nepal.

In 1964, Sonam Hisha Sherpa of Namche Bazaar, the capital of the Sherpa Khumbu region, was grazing his yak/cow crosses (the dzo) high on a mountain pasture with his men.

They heard loud whistling and bellowing as two Yeti hunted their cattle during the night. Terrified, they spent the night hiding in a cave, wondering if they would be next!

In the morning, Sonam and his men emerged to find that several head of their cattle had been killed and eaten!

☐ <u>I was here</u>

☐ <u>I saw a Yeti</u>

Don Whillans Sighting -
Annapurna, Nepal

In 1970, climber and Manchester plumber Don Whillans found and photographed strange footprints at his climbing team's temporary base camp.

Later that night, he observed a creature about a quarter of a mile away through binoculars for twenty minutes in bright moonlight.

Whillans described the creature as a powerful ape-like animal that bounded along on all fours and headed straight up a steep slope.

When he awoke in the morning, his stash of Mars bars had gone!

☐ I was here

☐ I saw a Yeti

Lhakpa Dolma Attack - Tengboche, Nepal

On July 11th, 1974, a young Sherpa woman named Lhakpa Dolma was attacked by a Yeti while tending her yaks near Tengboche, Nepal.

The creature dragged her to a nearby stream, where it dumped her before proceeding to kill her yaks. In this case, an official report was even filed, and the local police found the creature's tracks at the crime scene several days later.

Do you dare to capture a photo (or clip) of the legendary Yeti?

Caution: this creature is not always friendly!

☐ <u>I was here</u>

☐ <u>I saw a Yeti</u>

Taylor Tracks -
Barun Valley, Nepal.

In 1983, Himalayan conservationist Daniel C. Taylor and Himalayan natural historian Robert L. Fleming Jr. led a yeti expedition into Nepal's Barun Valley.

They discovered Yeti-like footprints, and some alleged large nests in trees that locals claimed were made by the Yeti.

They also examined two local Yeti skulls that were later identified as belonging to Asiatic black bear!

☐ <u>I was here</u>

☐ <u>I saw a Yeti</u>

Tishkov Sighting -
Mount Xixabangma, Tibet.

On September 22nd, 1991, Russian biologist Arkady Tishkov, part of the Soviet-Chinese Glaciological Expedition, watched a Yeti for nearly an hour on the southeastern slope of Mount Xixabangma in Tibet.

He tried to film the creature but was too far away. When he moved closer, the Yeti saw him and ran away.

Are you fast enough to catch a Yeti? Or, quiet enough to sneak up on one from behind?

☐ ___I was here___

☐ ___I saw a Yeti___

Destination Truth Tracks
Everest, Nepal.

In December 2007, American television presenter Joshua Gates and his team on Destination Truth discovered a series of humanoid-like footprints in the Everest region of Nepal.

Each footprint measured 13 inches in length, with five toes spanning 9.8 inches across. They also made casts of the prints.

Anthropologist Prof. Jeffrey Meldrum initially examined these tracks and believed they were too morphologically accurate to be man-made.

However, after further examination, he changed his mind.

☐ <u>I was here</u>

☐ <u>I saw a Yeti</u>

Stop and Consider...!

Before sharing any evidence you may have captured of the Yeti, it's essential to ensure it's GENUINE!

I know it's hard to believe, but there have been many fakes and frauds since Yeti-Fever took off in the mid-20th century!

Yeti Scalp -
Pangboche Monastery.

On 19 March 1954, the Daily Mail printed an article about expedition teams obtaining hair specimens from what was alleged to be a Yeti scalp found in the Pangboche Monastery.

The hair was analysed by Professor Frederic Wood Jones, an expert in human and comparative anatomy, who, after exhaustive testing, concluded that the hairs were not from a bear or anthropoid ape but instead from the shoulder of a coarse-haired hoofed animal.

Nevertheless, many monasteries throughout the Himalayas have similar alleged Yeti scalps that monks and monster hunters alike still revere!

Yeti Hand -
Pangboche Monastery, Nepal.

In 1960, Sir Edmund Hillary examined the mummified hand of a *'Yeti'* at Pangboche monastery and declared it a mix of human and animal.

However, Wildman Hunter-Peter Byrne later revealed that he had previously removed a thumb and phalanx from the hand with the monastery's permission and replaced them with human fingers.

The story takes on a Hollywood movie-like character, as we learn that the thumb and phalanx were smuggled out of the country with the assistance of actor James Stewart and his wife, Gloria; who hid the bones in her lingerie case!

Yeti DNA!
Royal Society Analysis.

In 2013, evolutionary biologist Charlotte Lindqvist was contacted by a film company working on a documentary about alleged Yeti evidence from the Himalayas.

Lindqvist and her team analyzed nine potential Yeti samples. Unfortunately, they found that a thigh bone belonged to a Tibetan brown bear, a hair from a mummified animal came from a Himalayan brown bear, and a tooth from a stuffed Yeti was from a domestic dog.

The other samples were also linked to Tibetan brown bears and Asian black bears.

Yeti Hair!
Eastern Bhutan.

In 2001, British zoologist Rob McCall claimed to have discovered Yeti hairs and claw marks in the hollow of a tree in eastern Bhutan.

McCall sent the hairs to geneticist Bryan Sykes at the Oxford Institute of Molecular Medicine, who thoroughly examined them and said, *"We found some DNA in it, but we don't know what it is. It's not a human, bear, or anything else we have so far been able to identify. We have never encountered DNA that we couldn't recognize before."*

Sadly, later analysis revealed that the hairs were from a brown bear and an Asiatic black bear.

Something to Remember!

This small sample of some of the most famous fakes and frauds should serve as a reminder that - The TRUTH always COMES OUT in the END!

I genuinely believe that an UNKNOWN ANIMAL is living in the Himalayas and that only GOOD RESEARCH undertaken by Citizen Scientists will lead to its DISCOVERY!

A crucial part of this process is accurately and objectively recording your data...

Field Notes...

Record your findings to pinpoint the perfect place to stake out the legendary Wildman of the Himalayas!

More Field Notes...

Did you remember to log the time and place where you saw the Abominable Snowman?

Even More Field Notes...

Did you see something unusual? Was there anyone else around? Don't forget to take their contact details to help verify your sighting!

Some More Field Notes...

Help your fellow researchers by recording what tools you used to spot the Yeti - a camera, a drone, a gamecam hanging from a tree.

Plans for the Future...

What will you do now that you're an Official Yeti Researcher? Why not write a blog, post a vlog, or even create your own Monster Hunting Manual?

Your Selfie with the Yeti

Many people have tried to capture an image of the Yeti. However, to this day, no one has snapped a genuine close-up photo.

Glue your selfie with the Yeti below:

Gotcha!!!
Now the Yeti has proof
that YOU exist!!

About the author:

Andy McGrath is a paranormal researcher and folklorist with over 25 + years of experience in the field.

A Speaker, Investigator, Podcaster (Beastly Theories) and Author (Beasts of Britain/Hairy Humanoids/Nessie: A Monster Kids Guide!)

He also hosts the television series - Weird Britain, which celebrates the histories, mysteries, folklore and fables of the British Isles!

<u>CAUTION!</u>

YETI: A MONSTER KIDS GUIDE! is intended solely to provide an overview of the history, mystery, landscape, and locations surrounding the Yeti legend and should not be used as a trail guide!

Any readers interested in visiting the Himalayas should carefully plan their trip and hire an experienced guide from a well-known and reputable provider.

It is also highly recommended that you do not travel alone and always take plenty of provisions, such as food, water, adequate clothing and navigational equipment on any expedition you plan to undertake.

Conditions in the Himalayas can change quickly, and inexperienced hikers can easily lose their bearings. Additionally, political conflicts and cultural norms in some of the lands adjoining this mountain range can be volatile.

Check Government advice (such as: *https://www.gov.uk/foreign-travel-advice*) before travelling to any new location, especially when attempting to cross any national border or tribal territory.

Remember! *"Hope for the best but prepare for the worst, and it won't take you by surprise!"*

DEAR RICKY !

YOU'RE A ARTIST, HUNTER
NOW !

(CONGRATULATIONS) !

Andy Warhol